D1480811

BOOK WORMS

# The Shape of the World

# Rectangles

**Dana Meachen Rau**

**Marshall Cavendish**
Benchmark
New York

Rectangles are big.

3

Rectangles are small.

Rectangles are for work.

Rectangles are for play.

9

Rectangles open.

11

Rectangles are in the mail.

Rectangles are in
the street.

Rectangles are in the yard.

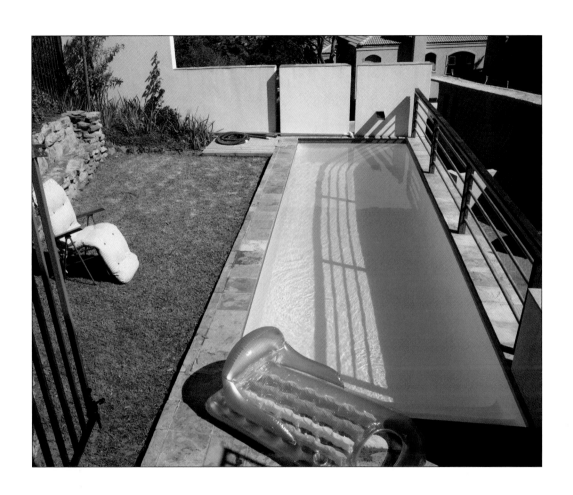

You can make a rectangle!

19

# Rectangles

bricks

door

jungle gym

letters

notebook

pool

skyscrapers

street sign

# Index

Page numbers in **boldface** are illustrations.

## About the Author

Dana Meachen Rau is an author, editor, and illustrator. A graduate of Trinity College in Hartford, Connecticut, she has written more than one hundred fifty books for children, including nonfiction, biographies, early readers, and historical fiction. She lives with her family in Burlington, Connecticut.

## Reading Consultants

Nanci Vargus, Ed.D. is an Assistant Professor of Elementary Education at the University of Indianapolis.

Beth Walker Gambro received her M.S. Ed. Reading from the University of St. Francis, Joliet, Illinois.

With thanks to Nanci Vargus, Ed.D. and
Beth Walker Gambro, reading consultants

Marshall Cavendish Benchmark
Marshall Cavendish
99 White Plains Road
Tarrytown, New York 10591-9001
www.marshallcavendish.us

Library of Congress Cataloging-in-Publication Data

Rau, Dana Meachen, 1971–
Rectangles / by Dana Meachen Rau.
p. cm. — (Bookworms. The shape of the world)
Summary: "Identifies rectangles in the world"—Provided by publisher.
Includes index.
ISBN-13: 978-0-7614-2282-2
ISBN-10: 0-7614-2282-X
1. Rectangles—Juvenile literature. 2. Parallelograms—Juvenile literature. 3. Geometry, Plane—Juvenile literature.
I. Title. II. Series.
QA482.R28 2006
516'.154—dc22
005032457

Photo Research by Anne Burns Images

Cover Photo by SuperStock/Comstock

The photographs in this book are used with permission and through the courtesy of:
Corbis: pp. 1, 7, 13, 20br, 21tl, 21tr Royalty Free; pp. 3, 21bl Charles E. Rotkin; pp. 11, 20tr Pete Leonard/zefa;
pp. 15, 21br Alan Schein/zefa; p. 20tl Dietrich Rose/zefa. Getty Images: pp. 9, 20bl.

Printed in Malaysia
1   3   5   6   4   2